BLACK AMERICANS OF DISTINCTION

IMPORTANT BLACK AMERICANS IN
Sports

John Allen

ReferencePoint
Press®

San Diego, CA

About the Author

John Allen is a writer who lives in Oklahoma City.

For more information, contact:
ReferencePoint Press, Inc.
PO Box 27779
San Diego, CA 92198
www.ReferencePointPress.com

LIBRARY OF CONGRESS CATALOGING-IN-PUBLICATION DATA

Names: Allen, John, 1957- author.
Title: Important Black Americans in sports / by John Allen.
Description: San Diego, CA : ReferencePoint Press, 2023. | Series: Black
  Americans of Distinction | Includes bibliographical references and
  index.
Identifiers: LCCN 2021051536 (print) | LCCN 2021051537 (ebook) | ISBN
  9781678202903 (Library Binding) | ISBN 9781678202910 (eBook)
Subjects: LCSH: African American athletes--Juvenile literature.
Classification: LCC GV697.A1 A436 2023 (print) | LCC GV697.A1 (ebook) |
  DDC 796.092/396073--dc23/eng/20220408
LC record available at https://lccn.loc.gov/2021051536
LC ebook record available at https://lccn.loc.gov/2021051537

CONTENTS

A Powerful Influence

In a packed stadium in Berlin, Germany, Jesse Owens crouched into his ready position. His every muscle and nerve were attuned to the moment. A pistol shot sent Owens and a number of international sprinters dashing down the track. Owens ran with his usual upright stride, an elegant combination of speed and power. A couple of runners tried to close the gap, but Owens crossed the finish line ahead of them in world-record time. His victory in the 200-meter race, however, did not please the host of the games. German chancellor Adolf Hitler had professed the superiority of the White, so-called Aryan, race. Yet the African American Owens had outpaced the field with ease. Owens won four gold medals overall, becoming the star of the 1936 Berlin Olympics. With his breakthrough performance, he also refuted Hitler's racist ideology. Like other great Black American athletes, he transcended his sport to show the importance of striving for greatness against all odds. "We all have dreams," he said later. "In order to make dreams come into reality, it takes an awful lot of determination, dedication, self-discipline and effort."[1]

Making a Statement for Human Rights

Owens is just one of a host of great Black athletes whose exploits have gone beyond the sporting world to influence American society and the struggle for human rights. On June 22, 1938, the boxer Joe Louis made a similar statement in front of seventy thousand fans in Yankee Stadium. It took Louis only two minutes to knock out Max Schmeling, Hitler's favorite German fighter, with a barrage of punches in the first round. At the time, Blacks still faced widespread discrimination in America, especially in the South, including segregated schools, neighborhood bans on housing, race-restricted restaurants and hotels, and off-limits picnic areas and swimming pools. But athletes like Owens and Louis showed that, given the opportunity to compete on an equal basis, they could reach the heights of excellence in their sports. Millions of Americans cheered their victories—and perhaps began to question their own prejudices as well.

> "We all have dreams. In order to make dreams come into reality, it takes an awful lot of determination, dedication, self-discipline and effort."[1]
>
> —Jesse Owens, 1936 Olympic gold medalist sprinter

In 1947 an even more seismic event rocked American sports. Jackie Robinson joined the Brooklyn Dodgers, becoming the first Black ballplayer in modern Major League Baseball. Robinson's immediate success—he won Rookie of the Year honors for his outstanding play—represented a breakthrough not only in sports but in the movement for civil rights. By crossing the color barrier in baseball, Robinson led the way for countless other Black athletes. In the 1950s future Hall of Fame baseball players such as Willie Mays and Hank Aaron followed Robinson's path to the major leagues. Teams in other professional sports leagues also began to sign African American players. By the 1960s Black stars such as Bill Russell and Wilt Chamberlain in pro basketball and Jim Brown in pro football had become household names for American sports fans.

Black athletes played a major role in the turbulent politics of the 1960s. In 1961 Russell led a boycott when several of his Black teammates on the Boston Celtics were refused service at a coffee shop in Lexington, Kentucky. Russell and the other Black players returned to Boston rather than play the scheduled game against

5

US track and field athlete Jesse Owens sets off on his gold medal–winning 200-meter run at the 1936 Berlin Olympic Games. Owens went on to win four gold medals, showing the world how one man could achieve greatness against all odds.

the St. Louis Hawks. Two years later Russell was a prominent participant in the March on Washington for civil rights, alongside Dr. Martin Luther King Jr. "It is the first time in four centuries that the American Negro can create his own history," Russell wrote at the time. "To be part of this is one of the most significant things that can happen."[2] Years later, in 2011, Russell received the Presidential Medal of Freedom from President Barack Obama.

Often, political protests by Black athletes rankled large segments of White America. In the 1968 Summer Olympics in Mexico City, African American sprinters Tommie Smith and John Carlos each raised a black-gloved fist on the medals podium during the playing of the US national anthem. Their show of support for the Black power movement caused a backlash among many White Americans and calls for the pair to be stripped of their medals. Recent protests in which National Football League and National Basketball Association (NBA) players have taken a knee during the anthem have been compared to Smith and Carlos's visual statement.

A Force for Change in Society

Beyond politics, Black American athletes have fought for the right to direct their own careers. In 1969 St. Louis Cardinals outfielder Curt Flood challenged the Major League Baseball reserve clause when he refused to accept a trade to the Philadelphia Phillies. The reserve clause had basically made players a team's property for life. Flood sued to end the reserve clause, which led to players becoming free agents when their contracts expired. In a similar vein, NBA stars like LeBron James and Kawhi Leonard have used free agency and personal leverage to join with other stars and create championship-caliber rosters on their own.

> "These athletes have simply begun to find their voices. These broader issues in the society are issues with a large scope."[3]
>
> —Harry Edwards, Black sociologist and professor at the University of California, Berkeley

Whether in politics, social commentary, entertainment, or fashion, today's Black athletes wield more power and influence in American society than ever before. Such influence brings with it new opportunities to promote positive change. "These athletes have simply begun to find their voices," says Black sociologist and University of California, Berkeley, professor Harry Edwards. "These broader issues in the society are issues with a large scope."[3]

CHAPTER ONE

Jackie Robinson: Major League Baseball Player

When Jackie Robinson came to bat for the Brooklyn Dodgers on April 18, 1947, his Major League Baseball (MLB) career was just a few days old. He had started slowly, going hitless in his first game. As the first Black player in the modern major leagues, Robinson faced pressure to succeed like no one else in baseball. He also had to endure a stream of abuse and racial slurs from fans and opposing players. He would even receive death threats in the mail. On this day a huge crowd of more than fifty thousand had showed up at New York's Polo Grounds to see Robinson go up against the hometown Giants. He tried to tune out all the chatter and focus on Giants pitcher Dave Koslo. With his usual smooth, level swing, Robinson stepped into a pitch and made contact that rang out with a sweet sound. The ball soared over the leftfield fence for his first home run as a major leaguer. While Robinson rounded the bases, a large group of Black fans in the bleachers rose up to cheer. Even many Giants fans applauded. But when he reached the Dodgers' dugout, not a single teammate offered to shake his hand. From the start, Robinson had to forge his path largely by himself. His achievement of breaking the MLB color barrier—and helping spur a widespread push for civil rights—made him a key figure in American history. But as Jimmy Cannon, a sports reporter for the *New York Post*, wrote at the time, "He is the loneliest man I have ever seen in sports."[4]

From Jim Crow Georgia to Pasadena

Jack Roosevelt Robinson was born on January 31, 1919, on plantation grounds in Cairo, Georgia. He was the youngest of five children. His father, Jerry Robinson, was a struggling sharecropper who abandoned the family when Jackie was still a child. Mallie Robinson, his mother, was the daughter of former slaves. After her husband left, Mallie decided to leave the segregated South for better prospects on the West Coast. She and the children traveled cross-country by automobile to Pasadena, California. There she bought a small house in a White neighborhood, worked long hours at various jobs, and raised the children by herself.

> "[Jackie Robinson] is the loneliest man I have ever seen in sports."[4]
>
> —Jimmy Cannon, sports reporter for the *New York Post*

Jackie hung out with some of the wilder kids and roamed the streets, stealing the occasional apple from a fruit stand. Nonetheless, he kept up with his schoolwork. In high school he began to excel in sports. Athletic ability ran in the Robinson family. Jackie's brother Mack made the 1936 Olympics team as a sprinter and won a silver medal in the 200-meter race at the Berlin Olympic Games, finishing second to fellow American Jesse Owens. Jackie made his own name at John Muir High School, earning letters in football, baseball, basketball, and track and field.

For college, he chose to stay close to home. He went first to Pasadena City College and then won a scholarship to the University of California, Los Angeles (UCLA). Robinson's eye-popping athletic exploits at UCLA soon became legendary. He performed especially well on the football gridiron, where his elusive running style made him a natural halfback. He won the national long-jump championship in 1940. He easily could have been an Olympic athlete had the games not been canceled during World War II. Ironically, his weakest sport in college was baseball, where he hit only .097 for the Bruins team.

When Robinson's eligibility for sports at UCLA ran out, he decided to leave school without getting his diploma. He was eager to pursue a professional career in sports. But first, in 1942 he was drafted into the US Army and sent to a segregated cavalry unit at Fort Riley in Kansas. He eventually rose to the rank of second lieutenant. In the army Robinson deplored how most Blacks were assigned the most menial jobs, such as cooking and cleaning. One day, when the driver of a military bus told him to take a seat in the back, Robinson refused. The incident led to a court-martial, but he ultimately transferred out of his unit with no penalty and an honorable discharge. Like Rosa Parks, whose similar refusal years later on a bus in Montgomery, Alabama, would energize the civil rights movement, Robinson would not back down from bigotry and discrimination.

A Plan to Integrate Baseball

Discrimination in baseball led to Robinson's first crack at being a professional ballplayer. In 1945 he joined the Kansas City Monarchs, a team in the Negro National League. At that time MLB team owners had an unwritten agreement, going back decades, not to sign Black players. As a result, Blacks with major-league ability had no choice but to play on all-Black teams in leagues organized by Black ownership. Negro League baseball featured many of the best players in the game, including future Hall of Famers like Josh Gibson, Cool Papa Bell, and Satchel Paige. Although the level of play was high, life for Negro League players was no bargain. Travel was constant, accommodations were second class if not worse, and salaries tended to be meager. Nonetheless, Robinson loved playing baseball for a living. He immediately stood out as one of the league's best young players.

Robinson soon caught the eye of Branch Rickey, the Brooklyn Dodgers' president and general manager. Rickey was one of

Jackie's Iconic Number 42

In Jackie Robinson's first season in the major leagues, he received many death threats, warning that he would be killed if he took the field at an opposing ballpark. After one such threat, a teammate suggested that every player on the Dodgers team should wear Robinson's number 42. That way, he said, they would not know who to target. Of course, every player on the team except Robinson was White. Robinson usually did not appreciate jokes about skin color, but that wisecrack made him smile.

Robinson would have been amazed to learn that in major league ballparks of the future, all the players would indeed be wearing his number. Beginning in 2004, baseball instituted one of the greatest ongoing tributes to any player. Each season on April 15, the day Robinson first took the field for the Brooklyn Dodgers and broke baseball's color barrier, every player in the major leagues wears Robinson's iconic number 42. As then-commissioner Bud Selig said in 2004, "By establishing April 15 as 'Jackie Robinson Day' throughout Major League Baseball, we are further ensuring that the incredible contributions and sacrifices he made—for baseball and society—will not be forgotten."

And when Hollywood produced a movie biography of Jackie in 2013 starring Chadwick Boseman, its title was simply *42*.

Quoted in Jack Baer, "Here's What MLB Is Doing for Jackie Robinson Day in 2021," Yahoo! Sports, April 15, 2021. http://sports.yahoo.com.

the best and most innovative front office men in baseball. When he headed the St. Louis Cardinals, he created the so-called farm system, in which minor league teams developed players for the major leagues. Although he believed in equality and social justice, he was also a hardheaded businessman. As the issue of civil rights for African Americans heated up in postwar America, civil rights groups and Black-owned newspapers were clamoring for integration. Rickey realized that the color barrier in baseball, America's most popular sport at the time, was not going to last. More importantly, he believed talented Black players could help the Dodgers win. He decided to move forward with a secret plan to sign a Black ballplayer.

The key to Rickey's plan was finding the right individual to break the color barrier. On the recommendation of Clyde Sukeforth, the Dodgers' top scout, Rickey summoned Robinson for an interview in his Brooklyn office. Waving his trademark cigar, Rickey did not sugarcoat the situation. He described all the abuse that the first Black player was bound to face. He even acted the part of racist fans and taunting ballplayers to see how Robinson would react. Jackie had to resist the urge to retaliate, Rickey told him, no matter how he was provoked. "Robinson, I'm looking for a ballplayer with guts enough *not* to fight back," Rickey said. "You've got to win this thing with hitting and throwing and fielding ground balls, nothing else!"[5] Robinson's composure during this emotional meeting convinced Rickey that he had found his man.

> "Robinson, I'm looking for a ballplayer with guts enough *not* to fight back. You've got to win this thing with hitting and throwing and fielding ground balls, nothing else!"[5]
>
> —Branch Rickey, Brooklyn Dodgers' president and general manager

Quashing a Racist Petition

On October 23, 1945, Robinson officially signed a contract with the Brooklyn Dodgers organization. His life would never be the same. In February 1946 he married his longtime sweetheart, Rachel, who would prove to be an invaluable support during his toughest times. One month later he reported to training camp with the Montreal Royals, the Dodgers' minor league club. He was the center of attention—for better or worse—wherever they played. For the season, he handled second base for the Royals and ended up as one of the team's best hitters.

The acid test came in 1947, when Robinson joined the Brooklyn Dodgers. At training camp in Daytona Beach, Florida,

Jackie Robinson is shown in 1949, the same year he won the National League's Most Valuable Player award and led the Brooklyn Dodgers to the World Series. Robinson's brilliant career and breaking of baseball's color barrier inspired many other athletes.

where anti-Black Jim Crow laws still ruled, he had to stay at a separate hotel from the rest of the team. There was talk that players on other teams would boycott games against the Dodgers, refusing to play against a Black ballplayer. Some of Robinson's own teammates asked to be traded. Star outfielder Dixie Walker, a southerner from Alabama, created a petition against Robinson's joining the team. However, on orders from Rickey, Dodgers manager Leo Durocher quashed the petition. "I don't care if the guy is yellow or black, or if he has stripes like a . . . zebra," Durocher told his players. "I'm the manager of this team and I say he plays."[6]

On opening day, April 15, 1947, 26,623 fans filed into Brooklyn's Ebbets Field. The fans witnessed history as Jackie Robinson, wearing number 42, trotted out to play first base for the Dodgers. Robinson failed to get a hit, but he scored the go-ahead run in the team's 5–3 victory over the Boston Braves. Some sportswriters, noting that attendance was several thousand short of a sellout, speculated that many fans had stayed home in protest of the Dodgers signing an African American player.

Slurs, Threats, and Physical Abuse

Robinson's first major challenges came on the team's initial road trip. Opposing fans and players alike let loose with racial slurs and taunts from the first inning. Pitchers threw fastballs within an inch of Robinson's head, sending him sprawling in the dirt. Runners would try to nail his foot with their spikes as they ran past first base. His teammates said nothing about the dirty tactics. It took tremendous self-control for Robinson to stay calm, resist fighting back, and focus on the game.

> "For one wild and rage-crazed minute, I thought, 'To hell with Mr. Rickey's noble experiment.'"[8]
>
> —Jackie Robinson

One of the worst venues was Philadelphia's Shibe Park. Before the series with the Phillies began, their manager, Ben Chapman, told his team to ride Robinson relentlessly from the bench and on the field. Bench jockeys dragged out the most offensive slurs: "We don't want you here, n— —! Go back to the bushes! They're waiting for you in the jungles, black boy!"[7] Chapman led the abuse. The Philadelphia fans also screamed insults throughout the game, as Rachel Robinson sat quietly seething in their midst. "For one wild and rage-crazed minute," Jackie later recalled, "I thought, 'To hell with Mr. Rickey's noble experiment.'"[8] Even worse lay ahead, however. Robinson began to receive death threats in the mail, some promising to kill not only him but also his wife and their infant son.

Turning the Season Around

Amid all the turmoil, Robinson's play was not up to his usual standard. But one month into the season, he began to turn things around. Suddenly, his bat came to life, as he smacked home runs and extra-base hits to all corners of the ballpark. He also made sparkling defensive plays at first base. His teammates finally seemed to realize that this rookie could lead them to a National League pennant. While not exactly friendly to Robinson, they began to accept him as a solid major league ballplayer. Some of the veterans, including Dixie Walker, offered him batting tips and advice on how to approach the best pitchers.

Robinson also brought a new aggressive brand of baseball that he had picked up in the Negro League. He laid down perfect bunts for base hits. On the base paths, he was not content to take a safe lead. He was constantly jumping around and feinting as if he were about to steal. He took every opportunity to get an extra base. His speed and daring kept the other team off balance. He was especially adept at the art of stealing home, one of baseball's most thrilling plays. For the season, Robinson stole twenty-nine bases, including three steals of home.

The Dodgers continued to win, blowing past the rival St. Louis Cardinals in the standings. They won the National League pennant by a comfortable margin. Brooklyn fans, including many proud African Americans, packed Ebbets Field and rocked the rafters with cheers for their new first baseman. Robinson ended up being named the National League Rookie of the Year. In his first World Series, he got some big hits, but the Dodgers fell to the New York Yankees in seven games. Nonetheless, Robinson had left no doubt that he belonged—that a Black ballplayer could excel against major league competition.

A Brilliant, Historic Career

Jackie Robinson went on to have a brilliant career with the Dodgers. In 1949, with Branch Rickey's restrictions on fighting back

Following his retirement from baseball in 1957, Jackie Robinson became vice president of a national coffee company. His main work, however, involved the continuing push for civil rights in America. He chaired the Freedom Fund Drive for the National Association for the Advancement of Colored People (NAACP), a million-dollar effort, and later was elected to the NAACP's board of directors. He also backed Martin Luther King Jr.'s nonviolent quest for social justice by working with King's Southern Christian Leadership Conference. The obstacles Robinson had overcome as Major League Baseball's first Black player earned him tremendous respect among African Americans throughout the nation.

However, Robinson's efforts met with less success during the racial unrest of the 1960s. He advocated for social change via the ballot box and Black-owned businesses. He rejected Black power groups like the Black Panthers that advocated racial separation and violent revolt. He urged Black voters to consider both parties, arguing that "it is not good policy for any minority to put all of their eggs in one political basket." But his own support for the Republican president Richard Nixon disappointed many Blacks, including the young. The heroic figure who had erased baseball's color line was widely dismissed as being politically out of touch.

Quoted in Michael G. Long, "Jackie Robinson Fought for a Racially Inclusive GOP," *Chicago Tribune*, January 30, 2019. www.chicagotribune.com.

finally lifted, Robinson's fiery spirit came to the fore. He won the league's Most Valuable Player award and led his team to the World Series once again. Robinson also opened doors for other gifted Black players. The Dodgers added catcher Roy Campanella and pitcher Don Newcombe to their formidable roster, and the American League became integrated when the Cleveland Indians signed outfielder Larry Doby. Soon nearly every team in both leagues featured Black players.

Throughout the early 1950s, the Dodgers dominated the National League only to lose to the Yankees in the World Series. Being a fierce competitor, Robinson longed to reverse the trend. But he also could respect great performances from his opponents. In 1952 he congratulated young Yankee slugger Mickey Mantle on his team's World Series victory. As Mantle recalled:

> After the game, Jackie Robinson came into our clubhouse and shook my hand. . . . I have to admit, I became a Jackie Robinson fan on the spot. . . . Here was a player who had without doubt suffered more abuse and more taunts and more hatred than any player in the history of the game. And he had made a special effort to compliment and encourage a young white kid from Oklahoma.[9]

In 1955 Jackie Robinson and the Dodgers got their revenge against the Yankees at last. Robinson set the tone in Game 1 when he stole home, sliding just under Yankee catcher Yogi Berra's desperate tag. Brooklyn prevailed in seven games for their first world championship.

Retirement and the Hall of Fame

Slowed by age and diabetes, Robinson retired after the 1956 season. For his career, he had hit .311, scored 972 runs, and racked up 200 stolen bases. But statistics pale before Jackie Robinson's real impact on baseball, race relations, and American society.

Robinson was voted into baseball's Hall of Fame in 1962, becoming the first Black player to be so honored. He spent the rest of his life working tirelessly for civil rights and Black opportunity. He died on October 24, 1972, at age fifty-three. Just the day before, Jackie, with Rachel at his side, had thrown out the first pitch at a World Series game in Cincinnati, Ohio. He made a point of urging MLB owners to break another color line and hire the first Black manager. To the end Jackie Robinson remained a crusader for change.

CHAPTER TWO

Muhammad Ali: Professional Boxer

On October 30, 1974, Muhammad Ali found himself pinned against the ropes of the spotlighted boxing ring. His opponent, George Foreman, the undefeated heavyweight champion of the world and a fearsome fighter, was pummeling Ali's body with blow after blow. Ali's trainer yelled at him to get away from the ropes, dance around the ring, and protect himself. But instead, Ali continued to retreat to the corners, absorbing Foreman's punches and leaning far back on the ropes to avoid blows to the face. Occasionally, Ali would flick his lightning left jab at Foreman's jaw. The writers at ringside could not believe what they were seeing. It was as if Ali wanted Foreman to continue whaling away at his arms and midsection. "I just knew no one could stand up to my punch," Foreman said later. "But Muhammad did. His taking those punches, I went away thinking, 'What is going on here? That's not supposed to happen.' That bothered me more than anything."[10]

It was a hot, muggy night, and swinging his heavily muscled arms over and over had exhausted Foreman. He lumbered after Ali with fading energy. By the eighth round, Ali saw his opening. This time when Foreman approached, Ali hit him with a trademark combination of punches. The last right cross sent Foreman wheeling awkwardly down to the canvas. Against all odds, Ali had won the so-called Rumble in the Jungle in the African nation of Zaire (now the Democratic Republic of the Congo), to the delight of thousands of Africans and fans all around the world. In a career filled with triumphs, setbacks, and controversy, it was Ali's most dramatic victory of all.

A Boxing Gym in Louisville

Muhammad Ali was born Cassius Marcellus Clay Jr. in Louisville, Kentucky, on January 17, 1942. His father, Cassius Marcellus Clay Sr., worked as a painter of signs and billboards. His mother, Odessa O'Grady Clay, held various jobs as a maid and cook. Cassius and his younger brother, Rudy, grew up in a segregated neighborhood amid Jim Crow laws that treated Blacks as second-class citizens. His mother recalled his frustration as a child at being refused the use of a department store's water fountain because of his race.

Dyslexia made schoolwork difficult for young Cassius, leading him to clown around with classmates to get attention. But he found another interest that changed his life. One day when Cassius was twelve, he and Rudy rode downtown on the bicycle they shared to run an errand. Having parked the bike on the sidewalk, the brothers returned to find it gone. Angrily, Cassius stormed inside the city community center to report the theft and then wandered into the basement. There he discovered a boxing gym filled with youngsters, overseen by a White police sergeant who loved the sport. The atmosphere of the gym—smelling of sweat and liniment, with kids punching a heavy bag, jumping rope, and sparring in a makeshift ring—appealed to him at once. Soon Cassius was going there regularly for boxing lessons.

As a teenager, Cassius showed great promise as a boxer. He grew to a height of 6 feet 3 inches (190.5 cm), with a long reach and a lean physique. He worked hard to increase his stamina and learned how to maneuver in the ring. Cassius impressed his early trainers with the speed of his hands. His style was eccentric, with his hands held very low as he danced and circled around his opponents in the ring. He would dodge punches by leaning backward, instead of moving his head from side to side like other boxers. Nonetheless, his coaches decided not to change his instinctive approach. Cassius went on to win a series of junior bouts, including six Kentucky Golden Gloves titles and two national Golden Gloves titles. At age eighteen he qualified for the US Olympic boxing team as a light heavyweight. In 1960 at the Olympics in Rome, Italy, he defeated a Polish fighter to win the gold medal.

In interviews, Cassius relied on his playful sense of humor to charm reporters. He made outrageous forecasts about his future in the ring and announced that he would one day be recognized as the Greatest of All Time. His biographer Jonathan Eig saw Cassius's emergence as a turning point in American sports. "It is a moment when we are poised between the old world of sports and the new world, when black athletes are going to become political figures," says Eig. "It's a moment when the world first discovers him and from there everything is about to get so much more fun and complicated."[11]

> "It is a moment when we are poised between the old world of sports and the new world, when black athletes are going to become political figures. It's a moment when the world first discovers him and from there everything is about to get so much more fun and complicated."[11]
>
> —Jonathan Eig, Ali's biographer, on Ali's emergence as a boxing champion

A Title Fight and a New Name

After the Olympics, Clay turned professional and embarked on a string of victories that made him the number one contender for the heavyweight title. Along the way, he taunted his opponents mercilessly, even predicting in which round they would fall—predictions that often proved correct. On February 24, 1964, he faced his toughest test so far: a title bout with Sonny Liston, the reigning heavyweight champion. Liston, who had spent time in prison and had ties to gangsters, intimidated his foes with a relentless, stalking style that had resulted in brutal knockouts. Oddsmak-

The Boxer and the Sportscaster

In the 1970s American sports produced few stranger pairings than Muhammad Ali and the sportscaster Howard Cosell. Ali was young, Black, handsome, quick-witted, and a convert to Islam, while Cosell was middle-aged, White, Jewish, and a former lawyer who had drifted into broadcasting. Early in Ali's career, Cosell realized that the young fighter possessed a charisma like no other athlete in the world. Interviewing Ali at his prefight training camps, Cosell would elicit the outrageous boasts and predictions, often in rhyme, that helped create Ali's legend. For his part, Ali saw Cosell as a willing accomplice in his mission to tweak the White establishment.

The pair had certain things in common too, including a habit of bombastic overstatement and a penchant for making enemies in the press. They traded quips in their interviews, but Cosell could be critical of Ali's praise of Black Muslim leader Elijah Muhammad or his racially demeaning outbursts against Black opponents like Joe Frazier. When Cosell died in April 1995, Ali paid tribute to his old friend. But he also joked, "I hope to meet him one day in the hereafter. I can hear Howard saying, 'Muhammad, you're not the man you used to be.'"

Quoted in Bob Raissman, "Muhammad Ali's Relationship with Howard Cosell Will Never Be Duplicated Ever Again," *New York Daily News*, June 9, 2016. www.nydailynews.com.

ers favored Liston over Clay by eight to one. Many fight fans, having grown weary of Clay's endless boasting, expected Liston to silence the young boxer whom some sportswriters called the Louisville Lip.

Yet Clay controlled the fight from the beginning. He peppered Liston with jabs, then backed off so that Liston's wild punches struck only air. The barrage of lefts and rights finally opened a deep gash above Liston's eye. Liston failed to answer the bell in the seventh round, giving Clay the title by technical knockout. He had stunned the boxing world.

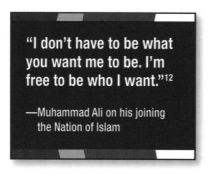

As the new heavyweight champion, Cassius Clay was now front-page news. And he used his new status to declare his independence. "I don't have to be what you want me to be," he told reporters. "I'm free to be who I want."[12] Shortly after his victory over Liston, Cassius Clay announced that he had joined the Nation of Islam, a Black separatist group led by Elijah Muhammad and based on the leader's version of Islamic teachings. Clay discarded what he called his slave name for a new name, Muhammad Ali.

Stripped of the Heavyweight Title

Ali's embrace of the Nation of Islam, which many Whites considered a dangerous group devoted to Black power, made him even more of a divisive figure. When he knocked out Liston in a rematch that lasted less than one round, some claimed the fight was fixed. Ali's habit of trash-talking and insulting his opponents repelled many old-school fight fans. At the same time, his popularity among young African Americans skyrocketed. With his movie-star good looks, razor-sharp wit, and willingness to defy the establishment, he became a folk hero to the Black community. Even so, his demands for respect sometimes crossed the line into cruelty. In a February 1967 bout with Black fighter Ernie Terrell, who had called him Clay in prefight interviews, Ali pummeled Terrell for fifteen bloody rounds. At one point Ali repeatedly demanded, "What's my name?"[13]

Two months later, on April 28, 1967, Ali officially refused to be inducted into the US Army, citing religious objections as a Muslim. At that time, with the United States involved in the Vietnam War, young males in America were being drafted into the military. Convicted of draft evasion, Ali faced a possible five-year prison sentence. Boxing's ruling boards, including the World Boxing Council, stripped him of his heavyweight title. Many state boxing organizations announced that they would no longer license any Ali fights. At the peak of his career, Ali seemed to be finished as a fighter.

The Fight of the Century

Ali's exile from boxing lasted three years, as his case worked its way through the appeal process. He spent time with his wife, Khalilah, and their four children. Tours of Europe, Asia, and Africa cemented his worldwide celebrity status despite the boxing ban. In 1970, when the Supreme Court reversed his conviction on draft evasion, Ali was able to return to the ring. A number of tune-up fights indicated that his boxing skills had diminished some. Still, Ali's reputation ensured high interest when he and Joe Frazier, the reigning heavyweight champion, signed for a title fight.

The bout was billed as the Fight of the Century. In his training sessions, Ali entertained reporters with his usual rhymes and boasting. Together with his old cornerman Bundini Brown, he promised that he would "float like a butterfly, sting like a bee."[14]

Muhammad Ali stands over fallen challenger Sonny Liston in their 1965 rematch. Ali, considered one of the greatest boxers in history, experienced triumphs, setbacks, and controversy in his career but won admiration for his messages of Black pride and resistance.

However, he also questioned Frazier's intelligence, called him an Uncle Tom, and offered up ugly racial slurs about his opponent. Frazier bristled at Ali's words and continued to call him "Clay." Despite the huge sums the two undefeated fighters were guaranteed—$2.5 million apiece—their meeting was not about money. It was personal.

On March 8, 1971, in a packed Madison Square Garden in New York City, Ali and Frazier staged what many experts consider the greatest fight in history. Ali danced around the ring in the early rounds, scoring with jabs and combinations. Frazier, hunched in his usual crouch, plowed forward to attack the retreating Ali. Then, in the fourteenth round, Frazier stunned the crowd by delivering a vicious left hook that knocked Ali to the canvas. Although Ali quickly got back on his feet, the blow was decisive. Frazier kept his title with a unanimous decision. Ali's jaw was grotesquely swollen, but he had earned new respect for his ability to take a punch.

Winning the Rumble in the Jungle

The public wanted a rematch between Ali and Frazier, but events took a detour. On March 31, 1973, Ali shockingly lost again, this time to Ken Norton. One of Norton's early round punches broke Ali's jaw, leaving him in excruciating pain for the rest of the fight. Some boxing observers questioned whether Ali would ever challenge for the heavyweight championship again. As for Frazier, he lost his title later in 1973 in brutal fashion to George Foreman. The match was no contest, as Foreman floored the champ six times in two rounds.

In 1974 Ali signed an agreement to meet Foreman for the heavyweight title. Promoter Don King arranged for the fight to be held in Kinshasa, Zaire, in Africa. Ali arrived in Kinshasa weeks early in order to train for what loomed as a major challenge. At age thirty-two, he no longer possessed the quick hands and feet that had enabled him to confuse his opponents. The twenty-five-year-old Foreman was as tall as Ali and had more punching power. Recalling how Foreman had demolished Joe Frazier,

An Activist for Positive Change

In his later years, despite being ravaged by Parkinson's disease, Muhammad Ali maintained his good humor and positive outlook as he traveled the world. He wanted to inspire people wherever he went to be respectful of their neighbors and to pursue their dreams. His patience in dealing with crowds of fans impressed even his former detractors. Ali especially enjoyed touring the nations of Africa and the Middle East, where his reputation as a brash, outspoken Black man made him an idol to millions.

Ali's decades of charity work raised large sums for Parkinson's disease research and the Special Olympics. In 1990 he used his international prestige to win the release of hostages in Iraq. In 1998 the United Nations named him a Messenger of Peace for his global outreach. In 2005 he was awarded the United States' Presidential Medal of Freedom. As then president Barack Obama said at Ali's funeral in June 2016, "He stood with King and Mandela; stood up when it was hard; spoke out when others wouldn't. . . . But Ali stood his ground. And his victory helped us get used to the America we recognize today."

Quoted in Natalie Escobar, "The Ties That Bind Muhammad Ali to the NFL Protests," *Smithsonian*, October 19, 2017. www.smithsonian.com.

some experts worried that Ali could be seriously hurt. His own entourage had their doubts. But Ali displayed no special concern in his training sessions. "This ain't nothing but another day in the dramatic life of Muhammad Ali," he said. "Do I look scared?"[15] Privately, he told his trainer, Angelo Dundee, he had a plan to handle Foreman.

The fight began at 4:00 a.m. in Kinshasa, so that it would be prime-time viewing in America. Sixty thousand fans filled the stadium, many chanting for their hero, Ali. In the second round, Ali tested his strategy by leaning far back on the ring's unusually loose ropes. The ropes helped Ali absorb Foreman's persistent blows. He felt sure that Foreman would think he was hurt and wear himself out with ineffective punches. When he spotted an opening, he would launch his own jabs. In the eighth round, Ali went on the attack and knocked out the exhausted Foreman. His risky plan had worked to perfection. In post-match interviews, Ali had a name for his strategy: the Rope-a-Dope.

Final Years with Parkinson's Disease

After his triumph in Kinshasa, Ali continued to fight. He liked the money, and he needed a lot of it to support his family, his training staff, his entourage, and various other friends and associates. And he loved the hoopla and attention. He fought Frazier twice more, in 1974 and 1975, and won both bouts. But the punishment he received did permanent damage. The third fight, dubbed the Thrilla in Manila for its site in the Philippines capital, proved especially brutal. Ali no longer had the speed or reflexes to avoid Frazier's punches. The fighters stood toe to toe, rocking each other with shot after shot. "It was like death," a battered Ali said after the fight. "Closest thing to dyin' that I know of."[16]

Reporters began to notice that Ali's speech had slowed, and he was slurring his words. Although he beat Leon Spinks in 1978 to win the heavyweight title for an unprecedented third time, his condition steadily got worse. He retired in 1981, after a final loss to Larry Holmes. His career record as a professional stood at 56 wins and 5 losses.

In 1984 Ali was diagnosed with Parkinson's disease, the result of countless blows to the head over more than two decades. He spoke in a whisper and shuffled when he walked. Yet Ali kept on touring in support of Black progress and

> "What I suffered physically was worth what I've accomplished in life. A man who is not courageous enough to take risks will never accomplish anything in life."[17]
>
> —Muhammad Ali at a news conference in 1984

human rights. He was said to be the most recognizable person on the planet. On July 19, 1996, Ali thrilled fans around the world when he lit the Olympic flame at the Atlanta Summer Olympic Games. Past controversies were forgotten at the sight of the former champion holding the torch high in his trembling hand.

Muhammad Ali died on June 3, 2016. Tributes poured in about his boxing mastery, his courage, his activism on behalf of Blacks worldwide, and his generosity. Despite the damage to his brain and body, he had no regrets. "What I suffered physically was worth what I've accomplished in life," he said at a news conference in 1984. "A man who is not courageous enough to take risks will never accomplish anything in life."[17]

CHAPTER THREE

Serena Williams: Professional Tennis Player

During the 2015 Wimbledon tennis championship in London, England, Serena Williams was in serious trouble. Her opponent, Victoria Azarenka of Belarus, had just sent a blistering forehand down the line to win the first set of their quarterfinals match. Azarenka always presented a unique challenge to Williams. She did not try to match Williams's power but instead used her skill as a counterpuncher to probe for openings and win long rallies. Williams was not at her best, missing her serves and sending routine shots wide. Yet she recovered to win the second set 6–2, setting the stage for a dramatic clincher. The third set featured epic rallies that called on both players to summon their best tennis. Finally, Williams's athleticism, pounding ground strokes, and lethal first serve earned her the victory.

She went on to defeat Russia's Maria Sharapova in the semifinals and a young Spaniard, Garbine Muguruza, in the finals to win her twenty-first major title. It was also the second time in her career she had won four Grand Slam events in a row, over two calendar years—the so-called Serena Slam. She had demonstrated once more not only her supreme skill but also her determination to be the best. "Serena Williams is your 2015 Wimbledon champion, and that's a sentence that should surprise precisely no one," observed tennis writer Chris Tognotti. "At 33, an age when most tennis players are on a severe decline, Williams remains one of the most dominant individual athletes in the world."[18]

An Education on the Public Courts

On September 26, 1981, Serena Williams was born in Saginaw, Michigan, to Oracene Price and Richard Williams. She was the youngest of five girls: full sister Venus and half sisters Yetunde, Lyndrea, and Isha. Richard, whose father had picked cotton in the South, insisted on better lives for his family. He moved them to the Los Angeles suburb of Compton, California, where he ran a private security firm amid pockets of gang activity. He claimed to have planned his youngest children's tennis future even before they were born. Seeing on TV one day the huge prize money paid to the winner of the French Open tennis tournament, he decided then and there that he would teach his children the game. And he started by taking lessons himself so he could serve as their instructor.

At age four Serena, with her older sister Venus, began to play tennis at some public courts not far from the Williams's house. Richard coached his daughters for two hours a day, instilling in them a passion for the game. Early on, he set a goal for the girls: to become champion professional tennis players. When they reached school age, he decided to homeschool them and devoted after-school (or before-school) hours to practice sessions on the tennis court. Some workouts began at 6:00 a.m.

The Williams sisters learned early that life in Compton could be perilous. Occasionally, shots rang out near the park where they practiced. Serena thought she was hearing firecrackers but her father made sure she knew she was hearing gunshots not firecrackers. Serena was nine when her father moved the family away from Compton to West Palm Beach, Florida. There the girls entered Rick Macci's tennis academy to refine their game. Macci and Richard had their battles about certain things, but Macci

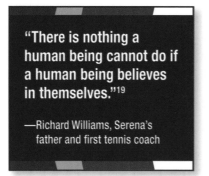
could not help but admire how Richard looked out for his daughters. For example, he pulled them out of junior tournaments when he felt that tennis was interfering with their schoolwork and their ability to play with friends like normal kids.

But one day, when twelve-year-old Venus announced that she was going to win five Wimbledon tournaments—which she went on to do—Richard had to smile. He knew his girls had the competitive fire. His dream of Serena and Venus achieving pro careers was not just a fantasy. As he said later, "There is nothing a human being cannot do if a human being believes in themselves."[19]

Meteoric Rise on the Pro Tour

In 1995 Serena became a professional tennis player at age fourteen. Venus had done the same the year before. The sisters created an immediate sensation on the pro tour. Both young women possessed uncanny athletic skills, including speed, strength, agility, and timing. Both employed a two-handed backhand per their father's instruction. Yet the sisters were far from looking like twins on the court. Venus took after her father, with a lean body and long arms and legs. Serena, by contrast, looked more like her mother, with a thicker frame that helped her deliver blazing serves and powerful ground strokes.

Reporters emphasized the impact that the Williams sisters could have on the sport. When they began their careers, few African Americans were competing at the highest level in tennis. Serena and Venus, with their electric, hard-hitting style of play, promised to shake things up on the tour. Many stories focused on the sisters' origins in Compton, compared to the country club background shared by many of their White opponents. Like Tiger Woods in professional golf, they seemed certain to inspire a new generation of Black players.

A Family Rivalry

One of the longest-running rivalries in tennis, dating back to 1998, is purely a family affair. Sisters Serena and Venus Williams have played each other thirty-one times in that span, with Serena holding a solid 19–12 advantage. Sixteen of their meetings have come in Grand Slam events. Early on, it looked as though Venus might be the more successful of the two. In their first match against each other, at the 1998 Australian Open, Venus won easily. She continued to hold the edge on her younger sister for several years. But when Serena fully developed her deadly first serve and overall power game, the rivalry shifted decisively in her favor.

The sisters' competitive fire ensures that each meeting is a treat for tennis fans. Their matches have featured some of the greatest athletic displays in women's tennis. Venus can take solace in the fact that she has defeated Serena more times than any other player. "The best part is (that) we bring out the best in each other," Serena told reporters at the 2018 US Open. "I know when I play her, I have to play some of my best tennis. She does, too."

Quoted in Nick McCarvel, "Venus and Serena's Decades-Long Rivalry: 5 Things to Know," Olympics, August 13, 2020. www.olympics.com.

After a brief learning period, Serena's rise in the rankings was meteoric. In January 1998 she won her first match in a Grand Slam event, beating the Romanian Irina Spirlea in the Australian Open. In February the Williams sisters won separate Women's Tennis Association tournaments on the same day, Serena in Paris and Venus in Oklahoma City. And on March 28 the two met in the finals of the Lipton Championships in Key Biscayne, Florida, with Venus winning 7–6, 6–1. Observers agreed that neither sister was at her best in the match. They said they preferred not to play each other, so that they could each root for the other's success. But by the end of the year, Serena and her sister had both cracked the top ten in international tennis rankings. "I wasn't expecting them so fast, you know?" said Spirlea. "Sometimes I'm in awe. They have something the others don't have."[20] Switzerland's Martina Hingis, the world's number one player, already was calling them the strongest opponents on tour.

An Historic Breakthrough at the US Open

Hingis was about to witness personally Serena Williams's breakthrough to greatness. On September 11, 1999, Williams met the top-seeded Hingis in the finals of the US Open in Flushing Meadows, New York. Reporters marveled at the youth of the finalists, with the eighteen-year-old Hingis, already the winner of five major

Serena Williams, winner of twenty-three Grand Slam singles titles, has dominated women's tennis. Her superb athleticism and her determination to excel in her sport have made her a role model for young women of color both in and out of tennis.

titles, facing the seventeen-year-old Williams. Yet the level of tennis on display was worthy of savvy veterans. Williams took charge from the start with her piercing serves and strong baseline game. She smacked topspin winners to the corners of the court, leaving Hingis to flail at the ball in vain. After winning the first set 6–3 and leading 4–0 in the second set, Williams had to fend off a late challenge by the talented Swiss player. But she prevailed in a tie-breaker to win her first Grand Slam event.

Serena Williams's rapid improvement caught many tennis experts by surprise. She had to go through a minefield of tough matches against ranked players on the way to the title. "Even though Richard Williams had already been making noise about how Serena ultimately was going to be the better player, better than Venus, we didn't think it was going to happen quite yet," says tennis journalist Steve Flink. "I just remember it really surprised me. A year or two later it wouldn't have, but I thought Martina [Hingis] was still going to have the edge at that stage in the final, with her experience."[21]

Suddenly Serena Williams stood atop the tennis world. She was the first Black female player to win the US Open since Althea Gibson in 1957. Her sister Venus, who had lost a close match in the semifinals to Hingis, was also destined for great things. The sisters provided reams of great copy for reporters, replying to questions with a disarming honesty and enthusiasm. When not practicing, they liked to shop and talk with friends. In many ways they were ordinary teenagers—who just happened to be the best young players in tennis.

The First Serena Slam

Serena's dominance of women's tennis was about to begin. But initially there were bumps along the way. In the 2001 US Open, she met Venus in the finals, the first time the Williams sisters had played a Grand Slam title match. The contest did not live up to the hype. Venus's easy win, 6–2, 6–4, left Serena furious with herself.

"She had a look that was totally different from the look Venus had when she lost," said former champion Pam Shriver. "Venus always thought if she had to lose, it might as well be to a family member. But Serena hated it more because it was her sister."[22]

Nonetheless, Serena got her revenge in a big way. Following her withdrawal from the 2002 Australian Open with an ankle injury, she caught fire during the rest of the year. In an inspired series of Grand Slam performances, she closed out the season by winning the French Open, Wimbledon, and the US Open. She then capped off the incredible streak by also winning the next major event, the 2003 Australian Open in January. That meant that Serena held all four major titles at once. It was not a true Grand Slam, since the four consecutive victories did not occur in the same calendar year. Yet tennis reporters celebrated her achievement by dubbing it the Serena Slam. Even more remarkable was the fact that she beat the same opponent in all four finals: her sister Venus.

Family Tragedy and a Rededication

On September 14, 2003, tragedy struck the Williams family. Serena's oldest half sister, Yetunde, was killed in a drive-by shooting in Compton. Listless and gripped by depression over her half sister's death and her parents' recent divorce, Serena Williams experienced the first slump of her career. She lost to Maria Sharapova in the 2004 Wimbledon final, the start of an extended slide. Although she won her second Australian Open title in 2005, her mind drifted away from tennis. Knee injuries kept her from working out, and she fell into poor condition. In 2006 her world ranking dipped to 81. Friends and veteran players feared that she was squandering her talent.

Later that year she traveled to the African nation of Ghana for a charity group promoting immunization for children. The trip, her first of many visits to Africa, changed her outlook and her life. As her mother recalls, "She came back a totally different person.

34

She fell in love with Africa. That helped her to refocus on her life and her career. Seeing where she came from, how we got to where we are now, seeing the ports where they shipped us off and the life of our people, that really changed her attitude about being a black woman."[23]

Upon her return, she hired a new trainer and slimmed down to playing weight. Her love for tennis started to come back. Unseeded in the 2007 Australian Open, she stunned the sports world by destroying Sharapova in the final. Williams's fierce desire to win would spell trouble for the world's top female players for years to come.

A Period of Dominance and Controversy

Most women in pro tennis have a relatively brief window during which they are at their prime. However, Williams maintained her dominance well into her thirties. In 2011, at age thirty-one, she became the oldest female tennis player to be ranked number one since computer rankings began in 1975. Her title at Wimbledon in 2015 was her fourth Grand Slam victory in a row, giving her an improbable second Serena Slam. She had developed her lightning serve into the best weapon in women's tennis, able to crease the line down the middle of the court or shoot off to the sideline. And she could still pound her ground strokes with the hardest hitters and track down balls most other players could never reach. Observers began to hail Serena Williams as one of the greatest athletes in American history, male or female.

But sometimes her competitive fire led to controversial outbursts on the court. In the semifinals of the 2009 US Open, Williams played the Belgian Kim Clijsters, a former champion who had revived her own game. Early in the match, Williams reacted to a bad shot by

Winning Grand Slam titles takes dedication, but Serena Williams enjoys a full life outside of the game. In 2017 she married Alexis Ohanian, cofounder of the online community site Reddit, and the couple have a daughter, Alexis Olympia. She has long been active as a goodwill ambassador for UNICEF, also known as the United Nations Children's Fund. With UNICEF, she has made several trips to Africa to support immunization efforts and build schools. Education has been a large part of her volunteer work. In 2014 she partnered with the Beyond the Boroughs National Scholarship Fund to help provide scholarships to students whose dream is to go to college.

Other issues close to Williams's heart are gun violence and violence against women. In remembrance of her half sister, who was killed in a gang-related shooting, she founded the Yetunde Price Resource Center, which works to help victims of violence overcome trauma. She has also combined her love of creating jewelry and fashion accessories with her activism and charity work. A handbag she designed was auctioned off to raise money for Purple Purse, a group that helps survivors of domestic violence. "Having a daughter changes our outlook on so many things in the world," she said in a 2018 interview. "The last year has really changed my already passionate mindset."

Quoted in Rose Minutaglio, "How Serena Williams's Daughter Inspired Her to Speak Out About Domestic Violence," *Elle*, October 2, 2018. www.elle.com.

smashing her racket on the court, earning her a warning. At the end of the match, a line judge called Williams for a foot fault, meaning her foot had touched the baseline on her serve. She exploded in anger. She threatened the lineswoman and showered her with ugly, expletive-filled abuse. The outburst brought a one-point penalty from the umpire. Since it was match point, the match went to Clijsters. US Open brass also fined Williams the maximum amount of $10,000. After making a defiant post-match statement to the press, she offered an apology to the lineswoman, Clijsters, and tennis fans. "I need to make it clear to all young people," she said, "that I handled myself inappropriately and it's not the way to act—win or lose, good call or bad call in any sport, in any manner."[24]

Chasing the All-Time Record

Williams's legion of fans forgave such outbursts. In the twilight of her career, they rooted for her to break a long-standing record in women's tennis: twenty-four Grand Slam victories, by Great Britain's Margaret Court. As of 2021 Williams needed just one more major win to tie Court. But at age forty, having lost a step or two in speed and with a young daughter, Alexis Olympia, to care for and dozens of outside interests, her prospects looked dim.

Nevertheless, Serena's astounding success on the tennis court has more than fulfilled her father's prophecies. She and Venus have dominated women's tennis for a generation. Between them, they have won thirty Grand Slam titles, including twelve Wimbledon victories. Serena's dominance from 2010 to 2019 was especially notable, since she won nearly 90 percent of her matches. Another part of the Williams sisters' legacy is the number of talented Black players they inspired to take up the game, including Naomi Osaka, who plays for Japan, and the young Americans Sloane Stephens and Coco Gauff. "It all starts with Venus and Serena," says Martin Blackman, general manager of player development at the United States Tennis Association. "That demonstration effect. The power of seeing two African-American girls with braids in the finals of the biggest tournaments in the world in a predominantly white sport. Just a huge impact that really can't be overstated."[25]

> "It all starts with Venus and Serena. That demonstration effect. The power of seeing two African-American girls with braids in the finals of the biggest tournaments in the world in a predominantly white sport. Just a huge impact that really can't be overstated."[25]
>
> —Martin Blackman, general manager of player development at the United States Tennis Association

CHAPTER FOUR

LeBron James: Professional Basketball Player

Late in the deciding Game 7 of the 2016 National Basketball Association (NBA) playoff finals in Oakland, California, LeBron James seized his chance to sway the outcome. His Cleveland Cavaliers were tied with the hometown Golden State Warriors. With two minutes to go, the Warriors' Andre Iguodala took a pass from Stephen Curry and came barreling down the lane to complete an easy layup. But James, who was just past half court, refused to give up on the play. He sprinted at full speed in pursuit, making up ground with each stride. As Iguodala released the ball, James leaped from behind him. With the ball an inch from the backboard, James batted it off the glass with his outstretched hand. To Iguodala—not to mention Warriors fans—it seemed as if James had appeared from nowhere.

James's stunning chase-down block was exactly the spark the Cavaliers needed to eke out the win, giving them the NBA title. It was one of the greatest defensive plays in playoff history. The block combined speed, timing, and extraordinary leaping ability, among the skills that James has used to dominate pro basketball for nearly two decades. It also demonstrated his fierce determination to succeed. "It's just another example of how he's just not going to let [his team] lose," says play-by-play announcer Mike Breen. "That was the thought as well after he blocked the shot: This guy is just not going to let this team lose tonight."[26]

Childhood in Ohio, from Struggles to Structure

LeBron James was born on December 30, 1984, in Akron, Ohio. His mother, Gloria (or Glo), was only sixteen when she had LeBron. Living in the family's small apartment then were Gloria's grandmother, mother, and two brothers—plus, according to Gloria, any friends who needed somewhere to stay. LeBron's father, Anthony McClelland, was a convicted felon with whom Gloria had had a casual relationship. As a young child, LeBron and his family moved from place to place. Money was always tight, and Gloria herself had problems with the law, although they were minor offenses. But family chaos often kept LeBron out of school. At age eight, he missed school for 100 out of 162 days.

Today James credits Frank Walker, his junior league football coach, for changing his life. Realizing that Gloria could not provide her son with a stable home environment, Walker took the boy into his own home. LeBron's life suddenly gained the structure it had sorely lacked. He went from a frequent no-show to the winner of the school attendance prize. "My life changed. I had shelter and food," says LeBron. "I'll never forget what the Walkers did for me, especially Frank. He doesn't get the recognition he deserves because he's real quiet, but he was the first one to give me a basketball and the first one to show a real interest."[27]

> "My life changed. I had shelter and food. I'll never forget what the Walkers did for me, especially Frank. He doesn't get the recognition he deserves because he's real quiet, but he was the first one to give me a basketball and the first one to show a real interest."[27]
>
> —LeBron James

Playing one-on-one with Walker's son in the backyard, LeBron soon displayed a flair for hoops. Walker noticed that LeBron paid close attention to his coaching tips and picked up things after only a couple of pointers. In addition, he began to grow, measuring 6 feet (183 cm) at age thirteen. His ball handling and passing skills developed rapidly, especially for someone with such size and strength. While still in junior high, LeBron had impressed several scouts as a future star. When he entered ninth grade at Akron's St. Vincent–St. Mary High School, at least one global sports agency inquired about representing him when he turned pro. LeBron led his small Catholic school to the Ohio state championship in his first year. Akron was abuzz about the prodigy in its midst.

From High School to the NBA

LeBron's national profile gave him the chance to meet, and play against, his idols. As a high school sophomore, he traveled to Chicago to play pickup games with Michael Jordan. The meeting convinced LeBron that he could compete at the highest levels of the sport. "A lot of players know how to play the game but they don't really know how to play the game, if you know what I mean," he said later. "They can put the ball in the hoop but I can see things before they even happen. A guy can make his teammates so much better. I learnt that from Jordan."[28] Soon afterward, *Sports Illustrated* magazine ran a cover story about LeBron James titled "The Chosen One."

In 2003, after graduating from high school, James became eligible for the NBA draft. The Cleveland Cavaliers, located just 37 miles (59.5 km) from his hometown, chose him with the number one pick. James's impact on the league was immediate. In the 2003–2004 season, he was named Rookie of the Year at age twenty, becoming the youngest player to win the award.

From the start, James could call upon a rare package of strength, power, and speed. He stood 6 feet 8 inches (203.2 cm) tall and weighed about 250 pounds (113.4 kg). He specialized in thunderous dunks that were celebrated on social media,

LeBron James regularly speaks out against racism and social ills. Like his heroes Muhammad Ali and Kareem Abdul-Jabbar, he has not hesitated to use his platform as a Black sports star to express his beliefs with strong language and actions. In 2012 James led his Miami Heat teammates to pose for a widely seen photo in hooded sweatshirts in tribute to Florida teen Trayvon Martin, who was shot and killed while wearing a hoodie. Two years later James denounced Los Angeles Clippers owner Donald Sterling for racist remarks he had made that were caught on tape. In Cleveland James got the team to wear warm-up shirts that said "I Can't Breathe"—referring to Eric Garner, a New York Black man who died from a police officer's chokehold.

More recently, James helped organize More Than a Vote, a group that fought alleged voter suppression by rallying Black voters in the 2020 presidential election. In recognition of his pursuit of social justice, James received the Muhammad Ali Legacy Award. In a *Sports Illustrated* essay, Abdul-Jabbar affirmed that the award was richly deserved. As he noted, "What is a hero but someone who stands up for those who can't?"

Kareem Abdul-Jabbar, "Meet Your 2020 Sportsperson of the Year Winners: LeBron James," *Sports Illustrated*, December 7, 2020. www.si.com.

but he could also fire pinpoint passes like a clever point guard. His physical skill and court savvy were already drawing comparisons to all-around stars like Jordan and the Los Angeles Lakers' Kobe Bryant.

A Controversial Decision

James's early career was filled with personal success. In only his second season, he was named to the East squad in the All-Star Game in Denver, Colorado. During the game, he thrilled the crowd with laser-accurate passes and a spectacular tomahawk dunk.

In the 2006–2007 season, he led the Cavaliers to the playoffs. James's first career playoff game against the Washington Wizards proved to be a triumph, as he amassed a triple-double—double figures in three statistical categories—with 32 points, 11 rebounds, and 11 assists. The next season, the Cavaliers won three playoff series to claim the Eastern Conference title. However, in the championship series James's heroics could not prevent a four-game sweep by the title-winning San Antonio Spurs. And in 2008–2009, despite winning the league's scoring title and Most Valuable Player (MVP) award, James again saw his championship dreams end in disappointment, as the Cavaliers fell to the Boston Celtics in the playoffs four games to three. When Cleveland lost to Boston once more the following year, James began to contemplate a change.

LeBron James (pictured in 2021) has dominated pro basketball for nearly two decades. He is known for his extraordinary speed, timing, and leaping ability as well as helping to usher in a new era of athlete activism both on and off the court.

Frustrated that the Cavaliers' front office had failed to surround him with sufficient talent, James revealed that he was considering leaving the Cavaliers. Fans and media pundits engaged in a frenzy of speculation about which franchise the game's greatest player might choose to join. The hype led to a made-for-TV special on ESPN called *The Decision*. On July 8, 2010, in an interview with sports journalist Jim Gray, James announced that he was signing with the Miami Heat. He was uniting with the Heat's Dwyane Wade, a close friend, and another friend, Chris Bosh, who came over from the Toronto Raptors. Together, they formed one of the first so-called superteams, organized via the players' agreement.

The dramatic buildup caused a backlash, with some of the media blasting the program as a silly extravagance and a product of James's ego. Asked if his race played a part in the negative reaction, James said, "I think so, at times. There's always—you know, a race factor."[29] Others worried that, following the trend, superstar free agents would simply band together, destroying the league's competitive balance. Michael Jordan admitted that he would never have joined together with his rivals that way. But no one could deny that the Miami Heat, led by LeBron James, would command attention like no other team in the league.

Winning Rings at Last

James took his game to another level with the Heat. Relieved of the need to focus on scoring, he distributed the ball to his teammates, especially the reliable Wade. In his first season in Miami, the team cruised to the finals but lost to the Dallas Mavericks and their star, Dirk Nowitzki. In 2011–2012, the Heat again fought through to the finals, where they met the upstart Oklahoma City Thunder and Kevin Durant. After an opening loss, James led his team to four straight victories and the championship. He not only won his first title, he also was named the finals MVP, averaging 28.6 points, 10.2 rebounds, and 7.4 assists for the series. For James, it seemed to vindicate his decision to leave Cleveland.

A School That Makes a Promise

LeBron James will never forget how the Walker family in Akron, Ohio, took him in as a boy with little hope and made him feel valued. That change in circumstances helped him discover his talent for basketball and led to a spectacular career. With his own situation in mind, in 2019 he opened the I Promise School in his hometown. The school attracts mostly Black elementary students whose low-income status and behavioral problems have put them at risk for not graduating. Using public education funds, plus an additional $600,000 from James, the school is able to hire additional teachers and have smaller class sizes. As a result, the students receive more personalized, hands-on learning. In the first year, their academic progress startled school officials. Ninety percent of the I Promise students reached or exceeded standards in reading and math. On average, they outperformed their age group throughout the district.

The school also provides services for parents, such as job-seeking advice, health services, and a barbershop. It all helps the children succeed. "These kids are doing an unbelievable job, better than we all expected," says James. "Now people are going to really understand the lack of education they had before they came to our school."

Quoted in Erica L. Green, "LeBron James Opened a School That Was Considered an Experiment. It's Showing Promise," *New York Times*, April 12, 2019. www.nytimes.com.

In 2013 the Heat returned to the finals for the third straight year, beating the San Antonio Spurs in a hard-fought seven games. Once again, James took home the MVP trophy as well as a championship ring. He had added a deadly three-point shot to his arsenal of offensive weapons, rendering him even more difficult to guard.

The Spurs turned the tables on the Heat in the 2014 finals, taking the series 4–1. With his contract up in Miami, James could not help thinking about his unfinished business in Cleveland. Although in 2010 Cavaliers owner Dan Gilbert had criticized him for leaving in a bitter public statement, James felt like he owed fans in Ohio another run at a championship. In July 2015 James signed a three-year deal to rejoin the Cavaliers.

A Comeback for the Ages

Back in a Cavaliers uniform, James immediately made the franchise a contender again. He carried the team to the 2016 finals against the Golden State Warriors, whose seventy-three regular season wins were the most in league history. James's performance against the Warriors may have been his most spectacular ever. Down three games to one, he decided to become the unstoppable scorer of his early years. He proceeded to drop forty-one points on the Warriors in Game 5, and then again in Game 6, to even the series. In the deciding contest, before a deafening crowd in Oakland's Oracle Arena, James brought back his all-around game. He skyed for rebounds, swished jumpers from the perimeter, and zipped passes to his teammates for layups. With the score tied late in the game, he swooped in from nowhere to swat away Andre Iguodala's layup attempt and energize the Cavaliers. Moments later, Cleveland's Kyrie Irving buried a three-pointer from the corner to seal the historic win. James still considers that series his finest as an NBA player. As he said two years later, "That one right there made me the greatest player of all time. . . . Everybody was talking about how [the Warriors] were the greatest team of all time, they were the greatest team ever assembled, and for us to come back, the way we came back in that fashion, I was like . . . you did something special."[30]

> "That one right there made me the greatest player of all time. . . . Everybody was talking about how [the Warriors] were the greatest team of all time . . . and for us to come back, the way we came back in that fashion, I was like . . . you did something special."[30]
>
> —LeBron James

He had also delivered a professional sports title to the long-suffering Cleveland fans for the first time in fifty-two years. After all the anger expended over his exit six years before—the jersey burnings and the crumpled posters—all was forgiven in Cleveland. Even Cavaliers owner Dan Gilbert had nothing but praise. "Words do not express the meaning and the feeling this accomplishment brought to the people of Northeast Ohio," said Gilbert. "None of this would have happened if LeBron James did not agree to come back home and lead the Cavaliers to the promised land."[31]

Another Title in Los Angeles

In 2018 James was on the move again, signing with the Los Angeles Lakers. By this time he had become one of the richest athletes in the world. According to the stock market website MarketWatch, his combined earnings and investments had made him the first billionaire among team sport American athletes. And in Los Angeles, he could not only play for a classic NBA franchise but also take advantage of new opportunities for business, entertainment, and activism.

Even though his 2018–2019 season was derailed by a groin injury, James soon proved his value to the Lakers. In the disrupted COVID-19 season of 2020, James joined with forward Anthony Davis to dominate the playoffs. His rejuvenated skills inside the COVID protection bubble at Florida's Walt Disney World helped lead the Lakers to the title. It was LeBron James's fourth championship overall, leaving him two short of his closest modern rival, Michael Jordan. But as former *New York Times* sports columnist William C. Rhoden said in 2020, "James is far from finished. Winning a fourth NBA title and leading a third team to a championship may not only be the pinnacle of his basketball career but in life, at 35, James is just getting started. There are so many more mountains to conquer."[32]

"James is far from finished. Winning a fourth NBA title and leading a third team to a championship may not only be the pinnacle of his basketball career but in life, at 35, James is just getting started. There are so many more mountains to conquer."[32]

—William C. Rhoden, former *New York Times* sports columnist

CHAPTER FIVE

Allyson Felix: Olympic Track Athlete

Rivalries bring out the best in athletes, pushing them to outdo themselves. On August 8, 2012, as Allyson Felix took the starting line at London's Olympic Stadium, she glanced over at Jamaica's Veronica Campbell-Brown. The last two Olympic Games had seen Campbell-Brown edge past Felix to take gold in the 200-meter race. It was Felix's dream to turn the tables this time and win the 200 meters, her favorite race distance. Three times she had won the 200-meter title in the World Championships but never an Olympic gold medal.

When the gun sounded, Felix exploded into a sprint. Her experience running the 100-meter race earlier that week—garnering a personal record though no medal—helped her reach top speed more quickly. Her characteristic long stride made her seem to glide down the track. In the home stretch, Felix relied on a burst that the other runners could not match. She won the gold in 21.88 seconds, afterward flashing her familiar smile and waving to the crowd. As for Campbell-Brown, she had faded to fourth place. After the race, Felix acknowledged how the rivalry with Campbell-Brown had inspired her. "To lose to her twice in Olympics Games has been tough but she's not like a horrible person so it's hard to hate her or anything like that," Felix remarked. "It's just that when we get in the races together we push each other."[33] The rivalry was just one more motivation Felix has employed to fashion one of the greatest careers in American track and field.

A Skinny Freshman with Amazing Speed

Allyson Michelle Felix was born in Los Angeles, California, on November 18, 1985. Her father, Paul Felix, presides as an ordained minister at a church in Sun Valley. Her mother, Marlean, a long-time elementary school teacher, instilled a love of learning in Allyson and her older brother, Wes. From her father Allyson inherited a deep faith that she has described as her reason for running.

At Los Angeles Baptist High School, Allyson was a gawky teen, all arms and legs, and so skinny that the other kids called her "chicken legs." But that thin physique held surprising potential. One day, when Allyson ran some timed 60-meter sprints with teammates on the school track, Coach Jonathan Patton had to double-check his stopwatch. Her times were startling. The skinny freshman possessed a natural acceleration that could not be taught. And when she worked out in the weight room, she amazed members of the football team by deadlifting 270 pounds (122.5 kg). Allyson's brother, Wes, shared her combination of speed and strength and was already a standout on his high school track team.

Allyson wasted no time demonstrating her sprinter's speed in high school meets. As a freshman, she excelled in the 200-meter race, placing seventh in the state meet for all of California. In her sophomore year, she captured second place in the Nike Indoor Nationals, one of the most prestigious track events in the United States. In the outdoor track season, she won her first state title, blazing through the 200 meters in 23.31 seconds and also finishing second in the 100 meters. In 2001 she got her first taste of international competition with Team USA at the World Youth Championships in Hungary. Allyson proved she belonged, taking gold in the 100-meter and medley relay.

Patton was proud of his star sprinter but not altogether surprised. "She does have a lot of God-given [physical] gifts," he said. "But it's that drive she has that separates her from a lot of other very talented sprinters. You can see it in the way she trains [on the track], in the weight room, in her diet, in the way she prepares for races and in the way she carries herself on race day. She just has that laser-like focus. She wants to not just win, but be her best."[34]

Turning Pro and Competing in the Olympics

During her stellar high school track career, Allyson won five state championship races against some of the nation's toughest competition. She also was named national girls High School Athlete of the Year by *Track & Field News*. The question then arose about which college she would choose. The University of Southern California had always seemed like the likely spot for her. However, she now had larger ambitions. She wanted to compete on the world stage, and she felt confident that she was ready. Thus, in 2003 eighteen-year-old Allyson Felix announced that she was turning professional and signing a contract with the sports shoe company Adidas. She would continue her education, with plans for a teaching career. But international track meets—and the Olympics—beckoned. These events offered her a chance to test herself against the best.

The 2004 US Olympic trials served as a coming-out party for Felix. Seeming to float above the track with her long strides, she won the 200-meter race and qualified for the US team. On August 25, 2004, at the Summer Olympics in Athens, Greece, Felix finished second to Jamaica's Veronica Campbell in the 200 meters to claim the silver medal. It was the first Olympic medal of her

A Loss That Led to a Victory

Coming into the 2008 Summer Olympics in Beijing, China, Allyson Felix ranked as the heavy favorite to win the gold in the 200-meter race, her personal favorite. She had left little doubt about her dominance in the 200 meters, beating her chief rival Veronica Campbell-Brown at the World Championships in 2005 and again in 2007. Everything seemed aligned for Felix's success.

However, at the starting gun in Beijing, Campbell-Brown exploded off the blocks. Instantly, Felix realized it would take her world-class speed to catch her rival. However, with only 20 meters to go, Felix saw that it was hopeless. She thought that she had done everything to prepare, but in a matter of seconds it all had come apart.

Nevertheless, the humbling loss led to a breakthrough success four years later. Campbell-Brown's amazing performance inspired Felix to work harder than ever. "I had to look at myself and figure out, am I going to keep doing this?" she said later. "Can I dissect every piece of my training, my lifting, my nutrition? Where is there space to grow? Am I going to do another four years when nothing is guaranteed? Like, how bad do you want it?"

Quoted in Tessa Nichols, "How Olympic Disappointment Ignited Allyson Felix," *Just Women's Sports*, October 29, 2020. www.justwomenssports.com.

career, and it also gave her a record time of 22.18 seconds in the under-twenty age category. In 2005 she flipped the script at the World Championships in Helsinki, Finland, sprinting to the gold ahead of Campbell.

The two rivals traded race wins in the 200 meters for years. In 2008 at the Beijing Summer Games, Felix considered herself at the top of her game. She had skipped some minor races in favor of a disciplined focus on training. She and her coach, Bob Kersee, would break down the race into segments and tailor her training to improve in each one. "Now, I'm feeling great and where I need to be," she said before the Beijing Olympics. "I'm just working on specific areas in my race now. I'm emphasizing my start and working on my curve running along with keeping up my endurance."[35]

In the Beijing 200-meter final, Felix's extra work paid off. She ran a personal-best time of 21.93 seconds. Yet Campbell-Brown, running in the next lane over, was reaching her own peak of excellence after an injury-filled season. She easily caught up to and blew past Felix to win by nearly two-tenths of a second. Felix was able to ease her disappointment some in the 4 x 400 meters relay, winning her first Olympic gold medal. Overall, she had impressed track experts with her explosive speed, quiet grit, and self-assurance, drawing predictions of even greater things in the future.

Breakthrough to Her First Individual Gold Medal

Felix's quest to finally win an individual Olympic gold medal in the 2012 London Games began in the US Olympic trials. She and Kersee knew that the 200-meter race required aggressive speed from the start, with no thought for pacing as in longer races. To get the proper muscle memory for an all-out sprint with a finishing kick, she felt she needed to qualify in the 100 meters as well. "I think my running style is a gift and a curse," she says. "It looks very fluid, you know, it's nice. But sometimes you have to get into that aggressive mode, and you need that quicker turnover."[36]

However, in the 100 meters at the US trials, she and her training partner, Jeneba Tarmoh, finished in a dead heat for third place and the last spot. Although Felix had already qualified for other races and would normally have given the spot to Tarmoh, she feared this might be her last chance at individual Olympic gold. Her friend Jackie Joyner-Kersee, a former

> "I think my running style is a gift and a curse. It looks very fluid, you know, it's nice. But sometimes you have to get into that aggressive mode, and you need that quicker turnover."[36]
>
> —Allyson Felix

champion herself, agreed with her, and USA Track & Field officials gave the last 100-meter spot to Felix.

As it turned out, her decision to stand firm likely made the difference. In London, although she failed to medal in the shorter race, she ran a personal best, giving her enormous confidence in her ability to accelerate. The 200-meter sprint unfolded just as

With her string of Olympic medals, Allyson Felix (shown in 2021) is the most decorated woman in US track and field history. She has also shown resilience and a willingness to speak out in the face of personal and professional adversity.

she had planned. Pumping her arms like pistons and maintaining speed with her long strides, she burst by the other runners, including Campbell-Brown, to win. It was Felix's first individual Olympic gold medal. She later added gold in two relays as well. She had established herself as one of the all-time great female sprinters. With her family in London to share in her achievement, it was Felix's ideal Olympic Games.

A Life-Threatening Childbirth

Entering her thirties, Felix had established a life routine that she loved. She split her hours between relaxing at home with her husband, Kenneth Ferguson, a former sprinter and hurdler, and workouts at the track. Her training schedule would ramp up as the annual World Championships approached or the Olympics loomed. In 2016 in the Summer Games at Rio de Janeiro, Brazil, she chalked up three more medals to her career total, including two more relay golds.

In 2018 Felix continued to compete even though she was four months pregnant. However, doctors found that her blood pressure was high and her baby's heart rate alarmingly slow. She was diagnosed with a severe case of preeclampsia, which can be life-threatening to both mother and child. At thirty-two weeks of pregnancy, Felix underwent an emergency C-section to deliver her daughter, Camryn. Following a number of days in the neonatal intensive care unit, Camryn was declared fully healthy and was able to go home with her parents.

The ordeal taught Felix about the high rate of maternal deaths in the United States. She found that African American women are three times more likely to die from pregnancy complications. "I'm an athlete. I take great care of my body and was in great health. I had a birthing plan. I was at one of the best hospitals in the country. There was no way anything could go wrong, right?" she says. "But my eyes were completely opened to the fact that

Some athletes feel empty and aimless when their careers are over. But Allyson Felix plans to have an extremely busy life once her sprinting days are behind her. As she reflected before the Tokyo Olympics in 2021, "This is my last time around. I feel sad for that, but also excited for what's to come."

One initiative that is close to her heart is helping pro athlete mothers pay child care costs when they travel. Along with sponsors Athleta and Women's Sport Foundation, Felix intends to distribute grants worth a total of $200,000 to athlete moms. She discovered the challenges of child care while competing when she traveled to the Olympics with her own daughter, Camryn.

Another project is creating her own shoe and lifestyle brand, called Saysh. The brand will offer products designed by women and for women. Felix made sure that the first Saysh offering was racing spikes, just like the ones she wore to win Olympic gold.

Quoted in Tyler Dragon, "Gabby Thomas Wins Women's 200 Meters at U.S. Olympic Trials with Second-Fastest Time Ever, Allyson Felix Fails to Qualify," *USA Today*, June 26, 2021. www.usatoday.com.

no one is immune from this reality and Black women face significantly higher risks—ones I wasn't really aware of and looking for."[37] Felix became determined to speak out about her experience and bring new attention to the problem.

Making History in Tokyo

Childbirth gave Felix a new challenge to motivate her training. In track and field circles, having a baby was thought to be a career-ending decision. Some questioned whether she could even make the US Olympic team. As Felix revved up her workouts in preparation for the COVID-19-delayed Tokyo Summer Olympics, she focused on proving the skeptics wrong.

At age thirty-five, she not only made the US team—marking her fifth Olympics berth—she also broke through to make history in Tokyo. In the semifinals of the 400-meter event, a race that calls for strategic pacing and a strong finishing kick, she fell back as one of the slower qualifiers. Nonetheless, the finals brought out a better performance. Although she did not win the race, her third-place finish gave her her first Olympic bronze medal. Moreover, it was the tenth medal of her career, tying her with the great Carl Lewis for American track and field medals. Immediately after the race, as she lay on the track looking up at the Tokyo night sky, she reflected on how she had fulfilled her most extravagant dreams of success.

> "My eyes were completely opened to the fact that no one is immune from this reality and Black woman face significantly higher risks [from childbirth]—ones I wasn't really aware of and looking for."[37]
>
> —Allyson Felix

But Felix was not through. She joined an all-star lineup of American female sprinters in the 4 x 400-meter relay. On the second leg, she ran 49.46 seconds, her season best, and widened the lead with her graceful strides. The team easily won the gold medal. With her eleventh Olympic medal, she had done what was once unthinkable and passed Lewis. Posing with her teammates, draped in a huge American flag and flashing her brilliant smile, Allyson Felix had nothing left to prove.

Introduction: A Powerful Influence

1. Quoted in Jesse Owens, Olympic Legend, "Quotes by Jesse Owens," 2021. www.jesseowens.com.
2. Quoted in Benyam Kidane, "Bill Russell: A Civil Rights Icon and NBA Trailblazer Whose Impact Is Still Felt to This Day," NBA, February 20, 2021. https://ca.nba.com.
3. Quoted in Sunni M. Khalid, "Black Athletes Have Always Been at the Forefront of the Struggle," The Undefeated, July 14, 2016. https://theundefeated.com.

Chapter One
Jackie Robinson: Major League Baseball Player

4. Quoted in Larry Schwartz, "A Hero for Generations," ESPN. www.espn.com.
5. Quoted in Peter Carlson, "Branch Rickey Hurls Barbed Insults at Jackie Robinson," HistoryNet, 2013. www.historynet.com.
6. Quoted in Baseball Almanac, "Leo Durocher Quotes." www.baseball-almanac.com.
7. Quoted in Todd Steven Burroughs, "That Time Jackie Robinson Was a Columnist for the *Pittsburgh Courier*," The Root, April 4, 2016. www.theroot.com.
8. Quoted in Marc Tracy, "69 Years Later, Philadelphia Apologizes to Jackie Robinson," *New York Times*, April 14, 2016. www.nytimes.com.
9. Quoted in Rick Weiner, "25 Most Beloved Players in Baseball History," Bleacher Report, June 7, 2012. https://bleacherreport.com.

Chapter Two
Muhammad Ali: Professional Boxer

10. Quoted in Josh Peter, "Revisiting 'the Rumble in the Jungle' 40 Years Later," *USA Today*, October 29, 2014. www.usatoday.com.
11. Quoted in International Olympic Committee, "Snapped: The Story Behind That Picture of Cassius Clay at Rome 1960," June 3, 2018. https://olympics.com.

12. Quoted in Johnny Smith and Randy Roberts, "Cassius X: Inside Cassius Clay's Conversion to Islam," The Undefeated, June 7, 2016. https://theundefeated.com.
13. Quoted in Bernard Fernandez, "Perception of Muhammad Ali Shifted After Cruel Battering of Ernie Terrell," The Ring, February 5, 2021. www.ringtv.com.
14. Quoted in Hilary Whiteman, "'Float Like a Butterfly, Sting Like a Bee': Best Quotes from Muhammad Ali," CNN, June 4, 2016, www.cnn.com.
15. Quoted in Jonathan Snowden, "Muhammad Ali's Greatest Fight: George Foreman and the Rumble in the Jungle," Bleacher Report, June 4, 2016. https://bleacherreport.com.
16. Quoted in Ken Jones, "Boxing: Ali v Frazier—'It Was like Death. Closest Thing to Dyin' That I Know Of,'" *The Independent* (London), July 20, 2013. www.independent.co.uk.
17. Quoted in Katie Reilly, "Muhammad Ali's Wit and Wisdom: 6 of His Best Quotes," *Time*, June 4, 2016. https://time.com.

Chapter Three
Serena Williams: Professional Tennis Player

18. Chris Tognotti, "What's All This 'Serena Slam' Stuff?," Bustle, July 11, 2015. www.bustle.com.
19. Quoted in Reeves Wiedeman, "Child's Play," *New Yorker*, June 2, 2014. www.newyorker.com.
20. Quoted in S.L. Price, "Who's Your Daddy?," *Vault/Sports Illustrated*, May 31, 1999. https://vault.si.com.
21. Quoted in Chris Oddo, "Serena vs. Hingis: When Teenage Grand Slam Finals Were the Norm," US Open, September 11, 2021. www.usopen.org.
22. Quoted in Alyssa Roenigk, "Road to 23: The Story of Serena's Path to Greatness," ESPN, March 27, 2020. www.espn.com.
23. Quoted in Roenigk, "Road to 23."
24. Quoted in *The Guardian* (Manchester, UK), "Serena Williams Apologises for Abusing Line Judge," September 14, 2009. www.theguardian.com.
25. Quoted in Christopher Clarey, "With More Black Women, U.S. Open Shows Serena and Venus Legacy," *New York Times*, September 4, 2020. www.nytimes.com.

Chapter Four
LeBron James: Professional Basketball Player

26. Quoted in Dave McMenamin, "When LeBron Swooped in and Changed the Course of Cavaliers' History," ESPN, June 27, 2016. www.espn.com.

27. Quoted in Lawrence Donegan, "America's Most Wanted," *The Guardian* (Manchester, UK), March 1, 2003. www.theguardian.com.

28. Quoted in Donegan, "America's Most Wanted."

29. Quoted in CNN, "LeBron James Says Race a Factor in Reaction to Miami Heat Announcement," September 30, 2010. www.cnn.com.

30. Quoted in Jace Evans, "LeBron James: Beating the Warriors for 2016 Title 'Made Me the Greatest Player of All Time,'" *USA Today*, December 30, 2018. www.usatoday.com.

31. Quoted in Ohm Youngmisuk, "LeBron James Agrees to Four-Year, 153.3 Million Deal with Lakers," ESPN, July 1, 2018. www.espn.com.

32. William C. Rhoden, "It's Time to End the LeBron James–Michael Jordan Debate," The Undefeated, October 12, 2020. https://the undefeated.com.

Chapter Five
Allyson Felix: Olympic Track Athlete

33. Quoted in Alison Wildey, "Athletics: Floating Felix Ends Long Wait for 200 Title," Reuters, August 8, 2012. www.reuters.com.

34. Quoted in John Ortega, "Key for Felix Is One-Track Mind," *Los Angeles Times*, June 19, 2002. www.latimes.com.

35. Allyson Felix, "I Know What to Expect and I'm Very Confident in My Training—IAAF Online Diaries," World Athletics, August 7, 2008. www.worldathletics.org.

36. Quoted in Sean Gregory, "How Getting Mean Got Allyson Felix Gold," *Time*, August 8, 2012. https://olympics.time.com.

37. Quoted in Danielle Campoamor, "Olympic Star Allyson Felix Speaks Out About Her Traumatic Birth Experience," *Today*, August 4, 2020. www.today.com.

FOR FURTHER RESEARCH

Books

Olivia Daniels, *Biography of Allyson Felix: The Most Honored Olympic Female Track and Field Athlete in History*. Self-published, 2021.

Jonathan Eig, *Ali: A Life*. New York: Houghton Mifflin Harcourt, 2018.

Michael G. Long, *42 Today: Jackie Robinson and His Legacy*. New York: New York University Press, 2021.

Hubert Walker, *LeBron James: Basketball Star*. Mendota Heights, MN: North Star Editions, 2021.

Dan Wetzel, *Epic Athletes: Serena Williams*. New York: Holt, 2019.

Internet Sources

Finn Cohen, "'Muhammad Ali' Explores the Many Layers of 'the Greatest,'" *New York Times*, September 9, 2021. www.nytimes.com.

Bradford William Davis, "Following Jackie Robinson's Commitment to Fighting Poverty Is the Best Way MLB Could Honor His Legacy," *New York Daily News*, April 15, 2020. www.nydailynews.com.

Erica L. Green, "LeBron James Opened a School That Was Considered an Experiment. It's Showing Promise," *New York Times*, April 12, 2019. www.nytimes.com.

Adam Kilgore, "Allyson Felix Leaves the Olympics with a Record Number of Medals and a Starry Next Generation," *Washington Post*, August 7, 2021. www.washingtonpost.com.

D'Arcy Maine, "For Serena Williams and Naomi Osaka, Nothing but Respect—and a Desire to Win," ESPN, February 16, 2021. www.espn.com.

Steve Wulf, "Athletes and Activism: The Long, Defiant History of Sports Protests," The Undefeated, January 30, 2019. https://theundefeated.com.

Websites

Anti-Defamation League (ADL)

www.adl.org

The ADL fights anti-Semitism and all forms of bigotry, defends demo-cratic ideals, and protects civil rights for all. Its website offers a resource library with a wealth of articles and other publications about religious, racial, and ethnic discrimination.

Black Women in Sport Foundation (BWSF)

www.blackwomeninsport.org

The BWSF is a nonprofit organization whose mission is to increase the involvement of Black women and girls in all aspects of sport, includ-ing athletics, coaching, and administration. The BWSF is unique in its ability to address the needs and dreams of girls and young women and in defining optimal ways to support them on their paths to lifelong achievement.

LeBron James Family Foundation

www.lebronjamesfamilyfoundation.org

The LeBron James Family Foundation invests its time, resources, and passion in creating generational change for the kids and families of James's hometown of Akron, Ohio. It focuses on the need for educa-tion through the I Promise School, a trendsetting model for urban public education.

National Association for the Advancement of Colored People (NAACP)

https://naacp.org

The NAACP works to disrupt inequality, dismantle racism, and accel-erate change in key areas. These include criminal justice, health care, education, climate, and the economy. For decades, the NAACP has tackled the toughest challenges related to social justice and civil rights.

INDEX

PICTURE CREDITS